Ctrl-Alt-Delete

Ctrl-Alt-Delete

Shannon D Maura Jr.

Charleston, SC
www.PalmettoPublishing.com

Ctrl-Alt-Delete

Hardcover ISBN: 978-1-64990-681-6
Paperback ISBN: 978-1-64990-682-3
eBook ISBN: 978-1-64990-683-0

Acknowledgment

I would like to acknowledge my long lost, but never forgotten friend, Evan Pittman. Writing has always been a way for me to express my thoughts and emotions. I have never been good with showing emotion or expressing how I feel, but I was always able to write my thoughts and feelings down. For years, I would write poems to get what I needed off my chest and most of the time I'd throw the poem away. Writing became very therapeutic for me, but I would never share with anyone. One day, I decided to share a poem I voice recorded with my friend, Evan Pittman. After he heard it, he immediately asked to hear more. After hearing more poems, he said that I needed to share these poems with the world. He believed that everything that he heard could be relatable to everyone and their life. I never took it seriously until he passed away. I was the last person to talk to him hours before he passed. To this day, I can still hear his voice and remember the last conversation we had. This book is a tribute to my long lost, but never forgotten friend, Evan Pittman. Continue to rest easy, my friend.

Table of Contents

Poetry

I told her I was into poetry and she said so am I.

I was taken back at first.

I hesitated, but I asked if she could share a couple lines.

I don't know if you express the same feelings as mine, but I write when I can't verbally express the feelings I keep inside.

Unbalanced on how the pen gives me balance, in a way that allows me to vocalize the feelings I keep confined.

I write about things that are never spoken.

Like how I wish I could rewind time to hear my brothers voice again.

Or how sometimes I feel like I have some demons deep down within.

I know this is new to us, but I never want to leave you in the blind.

I know myself better than mind, body, and soul.

I keep a lot of emotions pent in.

And without this pen,

I tend to implode into a deep hole of emotions one can call depression.

I just hope I haven't given you the wrong impression.

Message To My Son

Life is Beautiful.

And dreams make it more meaningful.

I couldn't dream of anything that makes my heart full, but when I see you I see me and there's no feeling comparable.

At once emotionless. Now I look into your eyes, I catch myself shedding tears.

Your toothless smile so innocent, praying I can protect you from any preconceived fears.

My heart feels for you. Like its never felt for anyone else before.

I want you to learn from me, but in time I want you to learn so much more.

Because life is a battlefield.

With each battle won the war is never done and you can always be better.

Just like I want better for you.

And I'd be lying if I said I wasn't afraid.

Because everything I do is a direct or indirect effect on you or on who you may or may not become.

Eventually like life or death, there is no in between on the boy you are to the man you will become.

And it's my job to lay that foundation.

Watch who I bring around,

Because the only difference between a garden and a graveyard, is what you put in the ground.

And one day you will see, life is hard because life is heavy,

But heavy is the head who holds the crown.

And one day you will be pronounced king.

And I want you to hold it ten toes down.

Friends With Benefits

No expectations, no disappointments.
We've all had friends with benefits.
I too, have a good friend with benefits,
But only our benefits aren't of the typical benefit.
We have something special, and that was evident.
The time we spent nothing of the physical, but it got a bit affectionate.
Sexually, that was never a thought or relevant.
She listened to me as I listened to her and sharing our heart was elegant.

I have never been one to conform.
One could call me a requisite.
I wish I could talk to a specialist.
We are solely friends, but nothing is definite.
Can anyone attest to my testament?
Can this even exist, or am I pessimist?
With pessimistic thoughts messing with my intelligence.

I have always tied loose ends, but let's not pretend.
If true love is finding your soul mate in your best friend,
Have I too found a soul mate in my best friend?

DM's (DM Slide)

Hey, how you feeling?
Overheard you were different.
Picture perfect, what's the difference?
Reminiscing on the times that I didn't.
Typed up a message.
I could have sent it.
This one sent 'cuz I'm sippin',
But please don't hold that against me.

Yea I admit it, picture perfect.
I can't fake it you come off intimidating.
Ask around I'm sure there is a number who can relate.

I would think I was equipped.
Although pretty, you seem adequate,
Which makes me digress, I admit.
Rambling, these DMs I haven't done it in a minute.

Please don't mind my admiration.
I'm really into mental stimulation,
Or mental penetration.
Outside in you look great
I wish you could relate.
Let's grab coffee or maybe brunch.
Let's see what really stimulates.

Casper Can You See Me

Casper can you see me?
Reminiscing on the love I used to get.
The love for an athlete, I can't forget.
I used to feel like no one could touch me.
Thousands of fans jumping out their seats.
Now I can barely stand on my own two feet.
I spend more time reminiscing on what I used to be.
Running down drunken tears, wishing I could run free.
I used to feel invincible.
Now I'm hurt, and I feel more and more invisible.

I remember when I felt like I was on top and no one could stop me.
Now I feel like Casper, can you see me?
Even in the mirror I'm confused.
The things I was into, now I'm not into.
Nothing seems to be the same.
There are days I wonder if people even remember the name.
It's hard to learn how to love my first love again.
I don't know if it's rebirth or born again,
But I pray to God I find that lost love.
Amen.

Walking Contradiction

They said if it was meant to be it will be.
I fell in love with fireflies. I swear I would never sell a dream,
But did I break my own heart thinking you were as solid as me?
In the mirror down on bending knees.
If the God in you is the God in me,
Why am I dealing with the devil I can only seem to be?

What is a heart if you left me heartbroken?
You created a monster. I remember I was soft spoken,
But you've had to be fucked over to learn, same token.
Now I cause hurt because I've been hurt, or heart broken.

I got premonitions of dying alone.
I'm a walking contradiction.
I want love, but fuck love. A constant repetition.
I been in love and out of love not all were my decision,
But what is love caught out of love?
A constant recollection.

Stabbed In The Back

I know everything isn't as we perceive it,
But the same cycle keeps on repeating.
It seems like people change with the seasons,
Or do shit for no reason.
Or is it at their own convenience?

I did you wrong?
Are you trying to get even?
Address, forgive and forget. That's what I believe in.
Two wrongs don't make right. That's what I've been preaching.

I don't know if it's a blessing or a curse. I can't seem to foresee it.
I have a big heart and the pain isn't relieving.
Internal pain. What is the treatment?
I been mentally drained not physically beaten.
I been stabbed in the back for whatever reason.

Our First Time

Flash backs reminiscing bout' our first time.
If I take this cookie does it mean that it's mine?
Contemplation, contemplating the good Lord knows I'm trying.
Love can get confusing if we ever cross that line.
Tempting, temptation running through my mind.
Should I take this cookie, or will I get declined?
If I take this cookie it would be her first time.

She must confess the soft touch of happiness as I touched her chest.
Under the covers, we embrace each other ducked off in the dark.

What happens next?
Our skin connect as I kiss her neck.
I have consent, but I admit I must repent.
Her subconscious telling her I'm a dog.

As I took a sip, I bit her lip.
She's steady trying to catch her grip.
I'm trying to catch a rip.
How did I finesse her out her drawers?

Three AM making love faces.
I feel her heart in sync with mine,
But her mind racing.
Life decisions I feel her heart, but she's contemplating.

She said is he mine?
Chills running up my spine .
Should I go right should I go left.

Ctrl-Alt-Delete

Trying to play it cool.
Does he knows this is my first time?

I'll be the first to admit it.
I don't want you to feel like a hit and quit.
I been around the block and somethings I regret,
But something about you this time is different.
When you ready, I'm ready and waiting I don't mind.

Who Am I

On my knees screaming why Lord?
I know that I am not all perfect, but I try hard.
I keep trying to tell myself that I'm not done yet.
The stress is holding me down like I'm still in debt.
If I didn't have a good support system me and my
maker would have already met.
I can hear the EKG steady beat Russian roulette.
Six feet under, Romeo but no Juliet.

Let's see where do we begin?
Steady looking for the three wise men.
While contemplating the unforgiven sin.
I feel like I been to hell and back and back again.
Contemplating suicide is like do or die.
Even though you know your faith is telling you suicide is eternal suicide.
I've been dancing with the devil. Wait, who am I?

Roses

I am an open book, but I wish it was closed.
Feeling exposed as a rose, yet clipped off, it's harder to keep its composure.
Outside in it shines but in time it's only looking for closure.
Outside in I shine, but inside I wish it would carry over.

You see I hurt from time to time and at times I feel like a fallen soldier.
Too much pride to push aside, I was never a push over.
But with time I find it harder and harder to stay sober.
Praying to God the good outweighs the bad when it's time to crossover.

Deception

Suicidal thoughts from suicidal feelings.
These tainted feelings are worth concealing.
Scars on my heart not so appealing.
These cards I was dealt. I wish I was dealing.
I wish I could let you in, not so much healing.

If I called you my nigga, that means you're my family.
Your problems are my problems, I don't have to understand it.
Right or wrong it's whatever, we'll handle it.

If you good, I'm good nothing else is my concern,
But you've had to been fucked over sometimes to have learned.
So I stand alone because the love I've shared I never got in return.

I stand alone, but alone isn't alone when you feel at home.
An offered heart is open to deception.
Taking shots to the head it may come off as aggression.
My thoughts have thoughts one can label a confession.
Slurred words trying to handle my depression,
But what's is depression when your depression gets depressing?

Recollection, a blur one can't label a confession.
Internal thoughts as I throw up my intestines.
We are characterized by our perfect imperfection.
We seek perfection, but perfection is indifferent direction.
Drugs will numb the pain another perfect imperfection.
Never let a nigga trick you out position.
It be the same chick wit' a reoccurring lesson.
Any love received is a reoccurring question.
All I ask Lord, is to protect me from deception.

Expression

My dad fucked up my communication skills.
I see him take it on the chin, but he never expressed how he feels.
Cards he never dealt, I never understood how he deals.
This is the reason why it's hard to express how I feel.
My good friend died but he was never killed.
I thought I had a friend, but it was never real.
My ex left a dent in my heart that I thought was steel.
I told her my inner thoughts, somethings never revealed.
I thought I was opening up so we could build,
But when we argued she threw it in my face like she aimed to kill.

In My Head

Sometimes I find it hard to figure out what to talk about.
I haven't achieved any achievements, filled with self-doubt.
I've been down to my last dollar, left alone to figure out.
So close to dealing weight.
I got a couple uncles who were trapped out.
Deep down I know that's not the answer,
But I'm left alone to figure out.

I be in and out of my head from time to time.
Like in and out my thoughts,
Who's fault but mine?
Why does time move so fast?
Life is like long division and I can't do the math.
If my past doesn't determine my future, why am I steady reliving the past?
I feel disproportional, but what is logical?
I don't know, cuz' I play stupid.

Show your hand and I'll show a portion.
See my hand, let me know what's my fortune.
But what's a hand to a hand when you count your misfortunes?
Inside out, I can't count. But I can count my distortments.

Insecure

To think girl I made you.
Or did I make you,
Insecure?
Insecure about the hoes I don't have.
Built from the insecurities of the hoes I once had.

Trust lost, wounds never heal.
They say love is a battlefield.
And I can only imagine how you deal.
I'm truly sorry for the ways I've made you feel,
But they say in time all wounds heal.
It sucks to have now realized that what we had was real.

Plot Twist

From make up to break ups to make up again.
We deviated from the plan and got back again.

All though a perfect imperfection.
I can't stand the sight of my own reflection.
Without you is like a lethal injection.
With news is it true or misconception?

Have you ever watched someone you love, be in love with someone else?
Kind of like being in a crowd and still feeling by yourself.

I'm solo in the game, but all I think about is you.
I told these hoes lies and made them sound true.
I did you wrong and I know you know you did me wrong too.
I didn't know who I was in life without you.

I thought we'd make it out alive.
I thought our dream would come true,
But with another plan. Me without you.
With a baby due in nine.
Na' that's not mine is it true?
I guess that was our time, our time overdue.

Due with a nigga I went to school with.
To think, this nigga we went to school with.
To think, I'd empty a whole clip.
To think, I never even shot shit,
But yea my mind it is pretty scattered.
From a heart that's pretty shattered.

Ctrl-Alt-Delete

Do you even care? Does it even matter?

Conversations with myself

Like how can I not be discouraged?

He did what I didn't have the courage,

But I thought I knew you better than a shotgun marriage.

I thought what we had could always be refurbished.

Now with a last name that's not mine how could you be so careless?

If your intent was to hurt me, mission accomplished.

I keep it together, but fallin' apart behind closed doors.

Why was I so immature?

I wasn't ready for the love you had in store.

And I have learned when it rains, yea when it rains it pours.

And in time yea, time is something we can't afford.

And yea, I did you wrong, but did you find what you were looking for?

I have never been the one to try to force shit, but the last chick I had I made her abort it.

Yea I was wrong, but a life without you I couldn't afford it,

But with you a new life that's not mine.

How should I be supportive?

I know in the past I have had a problem with commitment,

But what would you do if put in my position?

Now having his seed that's a whole 'nother commitment.

So fast, where was that in our love story unwritten?

You went from everything I envisioned to everything that didn't.

What Ifs Are Only Ifs

I hate when my thoughts have thoughts. I could fall abyss.
I hate when my gut knots have knots.
Some days I reminisce.
My lessons learned one could ball a fist.
If only my "if only's" happened as I sip a fifth.
I realized my "if only's" are only ifs.
I once believed in love. I could roll a spiff.
I realized true love is hit or miss.
You reap what you sew. God does exist.
He'll teach a lesson and some times the pain will subsist,
But to learn a lesson sometimes you have to reminisce.

Death

Life is pretty crazy, we all leave our troubled signs.
They say drugs aren't the answer, but they may ease a troubled mind.
They say drugs will numb the pain until you leave it all behind.

Drugs will make you hide behind the masks and makeup.
They say drugs will help you forget your troubles until you wake up.
They say drugs will make you forget until you forget to wake up.
I just hope you rest easy until we meet up.

Secondhand Emotion

Every day I pay homage to the God above,
But it seems like falling in love is that of a secondhand drug.
Leaving you itching to find those original feeling you were so fond of.
Searching for those first emotions you thought you found in someone else.
Triggered by the infectious feelings from that original love herself.
Or attempting to compel yourself not to relapse only with someone else.

That first love will make you feel like you can't get any higher,
Until you fall off fiending for that next supplier.
Attempting to try to figure out if love is what you truly desire.
Comparing what you have to what you had prier.
It's funny how your heart and your brain can conspire.
Knowing what's not good for you, but hoping your heart can inspire.

This drug called love can have you scared straight, contemplating Heaven and fate.
Wishing you could erase those feeling with a clean slate.
Love isn't just black or white.
I don't know if it's wrong or right or if it's fight or flight.
You're either running towards love or keeping out of sight.

I talk to God and in God I see myself.
I have learned you have to love oneself before.
you can let anyone love thyself.

Just When You Thought You Knew Me

Everything on the outside aren't as they appear on the in.
They say sticks and stones will break your bones,
But you never know what someone is going through within.
I may always have a smile, laugh, appear to live it up.
But more times than not,
I feel like I'm on the other side of luck.
When is it time to throw in the towel?
Enough is enough.
Unshown emotion, may appear to be tough,
But even a giant can be gentle when times get rough.

What's Going On

Without further ado,
Let's be as see through as possible so we can see things through
This seamless situation
Because I see us drifting away.
I don't want to throw what we have into an ocean of emotion of what could've been.
As of lately a lot of depression has set in,
Which has left me too confused to understand.
It's like your heart is now frozen,
When I was the one that commanded it to move.
You haven't been giving me the same energy
And lately my patience is running out of control.

Talk to me.
What's going on?
This heart you filled; I feel like our distance is digging another hole.
I don't want to go down the same road.
You say you miss me, but your actions are singing another song.
I may be tripping,
But I feel like our distance has caused a lot of friction between us.
I don't mean to fuss or fight
And I don't want to cause any more tension,
But it seems as though someone else has grabbed a bit of your attention.
Let's keep it a solid cause the pain of the truth is bearable,
But the pain of finding out the truth and not from you is unrepairable.

Our hearts used to be in sync.
And I know by continuing to ask you how you feel is demanding,
But I need to know.
Because this elephant in the room

Ctrl-Alt-Delete

Has left me alone to think all by myself.
And I can't fight for us when I feel like I'm the only one in the ring.
I just want things to go back to how they were.
You planted a seed in my soul
And you had to get through the weeds.
And I'd be damned if I make it easy for you to leave.

Natural

Weave track extensions you don't need that.
God made you beautiful, believe that.
I know the worlds got us conflicted.
What we know to what we see is contradicted.
The media shows beauty as explicit.
Living in the world of video vixen.
Whatever happened to beauty and tradition?
The Lord created you from his heart.
To realize your beauty shines from the start.
Men will always be men,
But there is nothing more attractive than a woman who loves the skin she's in.

Nylla Idoc

Have you ever been in love or felt love at first sight?
Jumped right in.
Feelings first,
Forgetting wrong from right.
Everything's soooo good,
Until you realize this is not a love song.

Fell in love with a chick in Miami.
Kicking back shots of patron she had me emotionally comfortable.
She had me opened up she had me emotionally vulnerable.
Expressing each other's hurt one could call it comparable,
But would we have the same connect if liquor wasn't a variable?

Talking about our past relationships and who we had relations wit'.
Shot after shot no time to babysit.
The time we spent, so elegant.
I thought I was in love I must admit,
But I was just a fuck, a short-term benefit.
She said this is Miami.
I thought that was evident.
Has my past caught up to my future in retrospect,
Or am I just dealing with some demons in my repent?

Ouhh how the tables have turned.
To think she's a woman I'm a little concerned.
To think back on all the bridges, I've burned.
Karmas a bitch I guess some feelings are earned.

Houston (Love)

A lot on my mind but nothing to say.
Sometimes I wish I wasn't so stuck in my ways.
A lot of trial and error I think I'm ready for change.
I thought I was running from love, but I was running your way.
Dawg meets dawg, I guess we are one in the same.
Wounds on my heart it gets hard to explain.
Once fuck love. Now you can carry my name.

Let's fuck the bullshit and cut to the chase.
These new-found feelings are hard to embrace.
Thought I'd never find love. I guess that was a phase.
If I give you my heart I'm done with the games.
Let's get over our fears face to face.
I'm trying to go the distance no quick race.
Let's learn from each other and do what it takes.

..... 3 months later

Shoot for the stars and try your luck.
I know a lot, but not enough.
I know enough to call your bluff.
I gave you my love.
I guess that's not enough.

Ha, you said you love me.
You throw around the word love as if it's subject pending to change.
There's no love lost eventually you get numb to the pain.
Were you ever all in or in enough to sustain?
But what is sustained if we barely remained?
Just another mental game of emotional charades.

I gave you my heart I thought that would count for something.
When it came to yours why so reluctant?
Why can't you keep it one hundred?
I thought it was I guess it wasn't.
You up and left me wondering.
You left me wantin'.
Anything for the tangible I want for nothin'.

On a date three days later but want to reminisce.
Drunk text have you fallin' abyss?
Your ups and downs I can't make to sense.
What's my past have to do with my future in my defense?
I truly care let's not pretend.
You want me then you don't want me. I been at your dispense.
Either you in or you out you've been on the fence.
I got love for you but not at your expense.

Cherish The
Ones You Love

Drowned in sorrow,
Here today gone tomorrow.
Time is precious, never borrowed.

Just because you're living doesn't mean you're alive.
Just like unrealized importance until you die.
It's crazy with time, out of time, time flies.

We lose sight in regard to time.
Until it's taken, what a crime.
Although memories forever shine.
Time not cherished whose fault but mine?

1/3/2018

What is your deepest fear?
It's only the third of the year
And I'm down bad shedding tears.

This shit is like a bad dream.
What do you mean
Somethings are better left unseen?

Call at four in the morning followed by a text.
I hesitated to check for fear of what would happened next.
Eventually may never come I must confess.
Things unsaid can be laid to rest.
Life is precious, but yet complex.

Just got off the phone with my dawg last night.
Four hours later he was gone no fight.
I turned to you when life seemed un-right.
You always made a bad situation seem alright.
Is it selfish of me to be upset that you followed the light?

The world knew you were a standup guy.
I know you're not supposed to question God, but why?
Why did my friend have to die?
Why was is it his turn to fly?
Why?

The Lord knew you were one hell of a man.
Something I will never understand.
So unexpected so unplanned.

You took me in as if I was one of the fam,
But damn Ev this wasn't the plan.

New Chapter

Over the years I feel like I have grown a lot
And you are part of the cause.
You have taken the good with the bad,
A long list of flaws.
I was on that immature boy tip.
We could list it all.

I have given you plenty of reasons to hate me with a lot of my actions,
But when I look in your eyes all I see is passion.
You stuck with me even through distractions.
And losing you I'd rather take a hundred lashes.
I could be down on my last ration,
But with you I have already cashed in.
You are more than a girlfriend.
I see you as more than my best friend.
Now having my son,
I hope it brings us even closer than we have been.

Shoot Your Shot

Hello my name is Shannon.
And my friends call me shan.
I couldn't help but to see you from across the way.
I apologize if you caught me starin'.
And excuse me if my words get to slurrin'.

But I think you're b-b-beautiful.
Even though I really admire you in the physical.
I really wouldn't mind getting to know your intellectual.

Please don't take this the wrong way,
But you know what they say everything that glitter ain't gold.
I want to look into your soul.
I want to undress your mind just to see if our energies intertwine.
Who knows we may age together that of fine wine.

I know what I'm saying sounds good but holdup.
There is a great potential that I might fuck your life up.
A little about me,
I know I ain't shit but I'm honest.
Honest to say honest I may step out on what we possess.
Needless to say, I would want you to stay.
Cuz' you'd be the first made conscience.

Nevertheless I've been working on myself.
And I think it's time to share it with someone else.
If we get to that level I know no one else could do you better.
Who knows, I might fuck your life up for the better.

Her Response

Thank you for your kind gestures.
Honestly, I admire your honesty.
And honestly, I'm not looking to change you, but I am looking for change.
We have all been around the block and back again.
I have never been one to conform so lets not pretend.
A lot of men see me as a piece of meat, I can't pretend.
My appearance is blinded by the light,
And most men don't care to know what's with in.
I don't want be another notch or a beneficial friend.
I'll ride for you if you ride for me.
I'll ride for you I'll ride till the end.

And you too are very attractive, don't think I didn't notice you.
It sounds like we are more than what meets the eye,
And I think you know this too.

You see I want intimacy but like you said nothing sexually.
You see in to me as I see in to you
And I'll do unto you as you do unto me.

I don't want to scare you, but I want something different.
Something that will last.
Something that will last. Last forever.
I'm not talking about marriage, but a bond that will endeavor.
A bond that will endeavor any weather
Or weather the storm.
I've never been one to confirm,
But maybe we can form something better.
I don't want to change you, but if you do change,

I hope we can change together…

If that's ok with you I'd be more than happy to give you my number.

I Pray

Yea thou I walk through the valley of the shadow of death.
I know I'm endowed with divine favor I know I'm blessed,
But I don't have too many friends to my right or my left.
Do some dirt and watch your "best friend" confess.
Letting people in I often digress.
Letting people in I often refuse.
A social introvert which makes me recluse.
Taking shots to the head more often abused.
Drugs to numb the pain more often misused.
We all been emotionally hurt or emotionally abused,
But to learn you have had to been messed over let's not get it confused.

My solitude is most often preferred.
Energy put out is energy returned,
But a lot of energy is much better observed.
You can say what you want most often I've heard.
You can say what you want trust has to be earned.
Couldn't tell you all the bridges I've burned.
Knowing most love shared was never returned.

I love my space but often I stare in space.
Somethings I couldn't face until I had to face.
Somethings I embraced I wish I had a brace.
Had a couple friends who caught a case.
And another couple friends that ran their race.
Life is what it is,
For fear I can't display.

Time

To agree or disagree.
I fear for nothing for fear I am free,
But I'm trapped or confined to some degree.
A lot of grievances I looked to the sky but couldn't see.
For some reasons I looked up to older people, but they looked up to me.

Ten toes I forever stand.
We have been taught or conditioned to try to understand,
But how do you understand something you can't understand.
Trying to figure out the figures, but life is never planned.

Time not cherished whose fault but mine.
You never know when it's your time to die.
Just in time, out of time, time flies.
I wish there was a blue print or guide, in regard to time.
'Cuz death is always calling to answer with no decline.

Love & Lust

Please don't take this the wrong way.
You see I say what I mean or do I mean what I say?
You said you're in love with me,
But I think you're in lust.
With experience I have had to adjust.
You see, with time I have found it's hard to trust.
We live in a world not love but lust.

I lived with both parents who would die for each other.
Grew up in a generation of people who say one thing and do another.
It took me a while to understand somethings I won't understand.

Some lessons learned are other lessons taught.
We have all been misleading or misled. Whose fault?
Selling dreams you don't at all believe.
We have all fallen victim or bought.
Because the thought of being in love tends to miscue your thought.
You thought you were in love, but you were only in love with the thought.